THE  OF

SCOTLAND

The Wee Book of Scotland
Dan Coxon

First published in 2000

by Jarrold Publishing, Whitefriars,
Norwich NR3 1TR

ISBN 0-7117-1508-4

Printed in Great Britain 2/01

Introduction

Scotland has attracted visitors for many years, but with the recent success of films such as *Braveheart* there has been a resurgence of interest in this most varied of countries. With its own Parliament now under way, Scotland is preparing to become even more prominent on the world stage. This little book is a collection of over 100 facts about this unique country – some are humorous, some are gruesome, some are bizarre and some are surprising, but all are interesting.

What's in a haggis?

Haggis is traditionally made from
minced sheep's intestines, beef suet,
oatmeal, onion, cayenne pepper and
nutmeg, stuffed into a sheep's stomach
and boiled for three hours.
Fortunately, haggis can now be
bought in the supermarket!

Tartan misconceptions

The word tartan originally referred to a type of material rather than a pattern, and was not unique to Scotland. Over the past two centuries, however, the Scots have undoubtedly made it their own!

Flower of Scotland

Although the thistle is popularly
associated with Scotland, the official
national flower is the bluebell.

Old Nessie

The oldest known recorded sighting of the Loch Ness Monster was made by the 7th-century monk Adamnan in his biography of the Christian missionary St Columba. Adamnan wrote that Columba subdued the beast when it attacked his followers.

Dead Nessie

In 1941 an Italian newspaper reported that the wartime bombing of Scotland had succeeded in killing the Loch Ness Monster!

Jacob's pillow

According to legend the infamous
Stone of Destiny was Jacob's pillow
when he had his dream of a ladder of
angels connecting heaven and earth.
Needless to say, this legend seems
to have little or no basis in fact.

First King of Scotland

The first King of a united Scotland is widely held to have been Kenneth MacAlpin, who united the Scots and Picts to become King of Scotland (as we know it) in 843 AD.

Making porridge …

Here is one of the many ways to prepare this classic Scottish dish. Boil ¹/₂ pint (225mls) of water, then slowly stir in 1oz (25g) of oatmeal. Simmer it gently for about 25 minutes, adding a little salt halfway through, then leave to stand for 2 minutes before eating.

… and serving it

Traditionally porridge is served in one bowl, with cold milk in another. Each spoonful of porridge is dipped into the milk before it is eaten – but on no account should any sugar be added!

Tartan misconceptions II

The common American usage of the word plaid to mean a tartan pattern seems to have developed from a misunderstanding – in Gaelic plaid simply means blanket.

Button it

The buttons on the sleeves of traditional Highland dress have their origins in the British army – they were introduced to stop soldiers wiping their noses on their sleeves!

Strangers in the night

It is considered lucky in Scotland
if your first visitor on New Year's Day
is a tall, dark man bearing a gift
of shortbread, a black bun –
or a lump of coal!

Worms that turned

According to legend, Scottish dragons were traditionally known as 'worms', but unlike their European counterparts they did not have wings.

Wee Scotland

Scotland covers approximately half as much land mass as England, about 30,500 square miles (79,000 sq km).

Wet Scotland

However, roughly 80% of Britain's coastline is in Scotland.

Wee Scotland II

The Scottish population accounts for approximately only 9% of the population of Britain, while London accounts for around 12%!

Fishy business

Over two-thirds of the United Kingdom's catches of fish and shellfish are made in Scottish waters.

Goal

The Scottish Football Association was founded in 1873 and is the second oldest football association in the world.

Funny old game

The Scottish side played in one of the oddest football matches ever during the qualifying rounds of the 1998 World Cup. When their Estonian opponents failed to show up, the Scots were forced to kick-off, even though there wasn't an opposition player to be seen on the pitch!

Scots abroad

There are now about
25,000,000 million people of Scottish
lineage living abroad, compared with
only 5,000,000 in Scotland itself!

Trust me, I'm a Scot

According to recent surveys most British people consider the Scottish accent to be the most trustworthy, and Sean Connery's voice to be the most trustworthy of all!

Scottish origins

One of the more unusual theories on the origin of the term 'Scot' is that it is derived from the name of Scota, an Egyptian princess who brought the Stone of Destiny across to Scotland.

Scottish origins II

An alternative claim states that
the word Scot originates from the
Latin word for pirates.

Looking for Atlantis

Tiree, the name given to the island in the Inner Hebrides, translates from Gaelic as 'the kingdom under the waves'.

Oa, Ae, Bu

There are three Scottish places
with only two letters in their names –
Oa (on Islay), Ae (in Dumfries
and Galloway) and Bu (on the
Orkney Isles).

Lords of invention

Scotland has produced
some remarkable inventors,
including John Logie Baird,
Alexander Graham Bell, James Watt
and Charles Macintosh…

King of comedy

…but it also produced 'the world's worst poet' – William McGonagall (c.1830–1902). McGonagall's poems are now celebrated throughout the world for their poor rhyming schemes, weak metaphors and outright banality!

Stealing destiny

There has been speculation that the Stone of Destiny, now in Edinburgh Castle, is not the original artefact. History has it that the original was carved, and not a plain sandstone block. Theory has it that monks fooled King Edward I when he stole the stone in 1296!

Stealing destiny II

In 1950 the Stone of Destiny was stolen from Westminster Abbey and hidden in Arbroath. Opinion is divided upon whether this was the action of Scottish nationalists or a daring band of students!

Shortbread

Shortbread is remarkably simple to make. Measure equal weights of plain flour, self-raising flour and butter, and half the amount of caster sugar. Cream the butter and sugar together, then add the sifted flours to produce a dough. Press into a baking tray and cook on a low heat for an hour.

First, last and ale-ways

Whilst Scotland may be more
famous for its whisky than for its beer,
the first recorded alcoholic drink
to have been produced in the country
was heather ale, believed to have
been made by the Picts.

Serious drinking

A 'joug', or Scots pint, is officially about
three Imperial pints, or 1.7 litres.

'Gardyloo!'

A popular cry in the 18th century –
'Gardyloo!' was a warning to anyone
walking beneath the crowded
tenement flats of Edinburgh's
Old Town. Literally it means
'beware of the water', but the slops
they emptied out into the streets
were not always so pleasant!

Bad Omens

According to Scottish tradition, the sound of a dog barking or howling in the night signals an impending death.

Wailing women

In Highland legend the mythical banshees were the spirits of women who had died in childbirth.

Wee, wee Book of Scotland

While this book may be small,
it has nothing on an edition of
Three Blind Mice published by
Gleniffer Press of Paisley in 1985,
which measured only
1.5 mm by 1.5 mm!

A very dead soul

Old King Cole, of nursery rhyme
fame, was killed when he went to
Scotland, by Fergus,
a Scottish chieftain.

Ghost of Lammermoor

Walter Scott's 'Bride of Lammermoor' was based on real events in Baldoon Castle, Dumfries, and to this day the bloodstained ghost of the bride, who was murdered or driven insane according to different versions of the tale, is said to haunt the castle.

Moor ghosts

Arnish Moor on the Isle of Lewis
is believed to have been haunted by
a figure dressed in 18th-century
clothing. Spookily, the body of a
similar figure was dug from the moor
in 1964, since when the appearances
of the ghost have ceased.

Highland games

The town of Ceres in Fife could claim to hold the oldest Highland Games in Scotland. Since 1314 the Ceres Games have been held each June to commemorate the safe return of Ceres men from the Battle of Bannockburn.

Highland fling

The term ceilidh, used now to mean an evening of traditional dance usually with live music, translates literally from Gaelic as 'visit' and was once used more generally to mean a social gathering.

The Scottish Play

One of Scotland's most famous literary figures, Macbeth, was a real historical figure who ruled the kingdom from 1040 until 1057. Contrary to Shakespeare's version of events, Macbeth did not die until three years after the battle of Dunsinane.

Military costumes

When Robert the Bruce's army
attacked the English fort at Kelso
it crept near to the fort's walls
disguised as a herd of cows!

The Munros I

'Munro' is a term for all
Scottish mountains over 3,000 feet
(915m). The term was coined after
the climber Sir Hugh Munro published
a set of tables listing all such peaks.

The Munros II

There are almost 300 Munros
in Scotland, including 12 peaks over
4,000 feet (1219m) above sea level.

The long and the tall

The longest loch in Scotland is
Loch Awe at 24 miles (38.4km) long,
although Loch Lomond has the largest
surface area and Loch Ness the largest
volume. Ben Nevis, in the Grampians,
is the highest mountain in Britain
at over 4,400 feet (1341m).

A thorny issue

The thistle first officially appeared
as the Scottish emblem on coinage
around 1470, during the reign
of James III.

Written in stone

Carvings of cacti and Indian corn inside Roslin Chapel, on the outskirts of Edinburgh, present fairly convincing evidence that the founder's grandfather, Prince Henry of Orkney, set foot in the New World a full century before Columbus!

Watch your back

Pontius Pilate is said to have been a Scot. According to some, he was born in Perthshire when his father was posted there on military service.

Never trust a politician

William Brodie is said to have
inspired R. L. Stevenson's novel
*The Strange Case of Dr Jekyll
and Mr Hyde*. An Edinburgh town
councillor and cabinet-maker by day,
by night Brodie was the leader of a
gang of thieves and a compulsive
gambler. He was eventually executed
for his crimes in 1788.

Banned sport

In 1457 James II tried, unsuccessfully, to ban football in Scotland, a decision that would not be any more popular today!

Royal and ancient

It is generally recognised that Scotland gave golf to the rest of the world, and that the Royal and Ancient Golf Club in St Andrews is the home of golf. Although the club was not established until 1754, it is thought that the game was played on the links at St Andrews as long ago as the 12th century.

Scots descendants

Although she never sat on the English throne, Mary Queen of Scots is the ancestor of all the English monarchs who followed her.

Heart of Scotland

The heart of Robert the Bruce is reputedly buried in Melrose Abbey, in the Borders.

Tartan invention

Claims have been made that the modern kilt was devised by an Englishman named Rawlinson who was in charge of an iron-smelting works in Lochaber. Needless to say, the Scots vigorously deny this!

Tartan etiquette

Whilst it is currently considered fashionable to wear your family's tartan, this habit has little historical basis and it is better to let good taste be your guide. However, to fabricate a link to a family with whom you have no connection is considered a serious *faux pas* in some circles!

Botanic record breaker

The Royal Botanic Garden in Edinburgh boasts the world's largest collection of rhododendrons…

Botanic record breaker II

…the tallest glasshouse in Britain…

Botanic record breaker III

…and used to boast the tallest palm tree in Britain, until it was chopped down in 1987.
Still, two out of three isn't bad!

Headless drummer boy

Edinburgh Castle is haunted
by the ghost of a headless drummer
who is said to appear only when the
castle is about to be besieged. His first
recorded appearance was in 1650 just
before Cromwell attacked.

Another apparition

Dalry House in Edinburgh is reputedly haunted by a one-armed ghost. The spirit is supposedly of John Chiesly, a man who had his arm chopped off as punishment for shooting Sir George Lockhart. Rumour has it, though, that the ghost is 'armless!

Bride's pie

A recipe has survived from
18th-century Edinburgh for
'Bride's pie', an odd mixture of calf's
feet, apples, raisins, cinnamon,
brandy and champagne.

Rumbledethumps

This is an alternative to neeps'n'tatties. Fry some cabbage (preferably kale) in a little oil and mix in with mashed potatoes. For an interesting variation, add some chopped chives to the potatoes before mashing them.

Great Scot

Sean Connery has appeared in over 60
films to date, including seven
appearances as Ian Fleming's
hero James Bond.

Highlander

The 1986 film *Highlander* stars French
actor Christopher Lambert as the
eponymous highlander, and native Scot
Sean Connery as a Spaniard!

Irish Braveheart

The 1996 film *Braveheart* gave an important boost to the Scottish tourist industry, even though the majority of scenes were shot in Ireland!

Falling on deaf ears

In 1899 a Chicago judge ruled
that the bagpipes were not a
musical instrument.

The Lighthouse Family

R. L. Stevenson's ancestors are almost as famous as he is, but for feats of engineering rather than the written word. In particular they designed and built a large number of Scotland's lighthouses, causing the famous author to write that he 'might write books till 1900 and not serve humanity so well'.

The auld enemy

Despite being the two oldest
international football teams in the
world, England and Scotland
have never played each other
in the World Cup finals.

The auld enemy II

The Scottish rugby union side was so confident of a victory over England in 1897 that it didn't even bother taking the Calcutta Cup along to the match.
Needless to say, the English side won 12-3!

Place names

Scotland's longest
single-word place name is
Coignafeuinternich in Inverness-shire.
The shortest is I,
the Gaelic name for Iona!

East and west

Edinburgh is on the same line of
latitude as Moscow!

Start them young

It was a practice of Scottish midwives
to sometimes place whisky in a
new-born baby's mouth to
ward off the evil eye!

Hubble, bubble

One of Scotland's most notorious witches was Isobel Gowdie, who claimed in her trial in 1662 that she had made a pact with the devil fifteen years earlier which had enabled her to fly and turn into a cat!

The last witch

Scotland's last witch trial was in 1722, when Janet Horne was sentenced to death by burning in a tar barrel.

The King's Visit

Prestwick Airport proudly lays claim
to being the only place in Britain to
have been visited by Elvis Presley,
the visit taking place on
2 March 1960.

Scotsman on the moon

Neil Armstrong, the first man to walk on the moon, carried a piece of Armstrong clan tartan with him on his historic voyage!

The real St Andrew

St Andrew, the patron saint of Scotland, was one of the first of the disciples to follow Jesus and died in Greece around 60 AD. He is also the patron saint of Greece and Russia.

Tartan armies

The first book on clan tartans did not appear until 1819 and listed 100 key patterns, but since then the number of officially recognised tartans has risen to over 2,000 – and is still growing!

Hazardous duke

The Duke of Atholl is officially the only person in the United Kingdom allowed to raise a private army.

School for Dunces

The word dunce is thought to come from the term for the followers of Duns Scotus, a renowned philosopher born in Duns around 1265.
The pedantry of their school of thought led to their name being equated with stupidity!

English haggis

Contrary to popular belief haggis was enjoyed in England as well as Scotland up until the end of the 18th century, and only acquired its particularly Scottish identity from the Robert Burns poem 'To a Haggis'.

Haggis and ouzo

A dish similar to haggis is mentioned by Athanaeus in his writing on 2nd-century Greece!

Neeps 'n' tatties

This is the classic accompaniment to haggis, and is remarkably simple to make. Just peel, chop and boil roughly equal quantities of potato and turnip or swede, and then drain and mash them together with a little butter and seasoning. Make sure you don't forget the haggis!

Islands and highlands

Scotland has 790 islands,
of which only 130 are inhabited.
At the other end of the scale, roughly
65% of the Scottish land mass sits at
over 400 feet (122m) above sea level.

Nova Scotia

The area of North America now known as Nova Scotia was colonised by the Scots in 1625, but they were forced out in 1632 by the French, who had a prior claim to the region and named it 'Acadia'. It only reverted to Nova Scotia in the 18th century, following the British conquest of French Canada.

Going underground

Beneath the City Chambers in Edinburgh lies Mary King's Close, a street that was closed off and sealed up following the plague of 1645 and has since been built over. Today, tours of the close are conducted for tourists, and a number of ghostly sightings have been recorded.

In the hot seat

Arthur's Seat in Edinburgh's
Holyrood Park is all that remains of
the Edinburgh volcano, which erupted
around 325,000,000 years ago.
The volcano also included the
Castle Rock and Calton Hill.

An easy win

In 1885 an incredible score was recorded in the Scottish Football Association Cup when Arbroath beat Bon Accord 36-0!

Football grounds

The first England vs Scotland football match was played in 1872 – on the West of Scotland Cricket Ground!

The Forth Bridge

The Forth Railway Bridge took seven years to construct, and consists of 54,000 tons of steel held together by over 8,000,000 rivets!

Scottish cold war

Not only does Scotland have its own
Washington, near Coupar Angus,
but it also has a village called Moscow
just north-east of Kilmarnock!

Moving the borders

Originally Castle Rock in Edinburgh marked Scotland's border with England. Following Malcolm I's victory over the Northumbrians in 1018 the border was moved south to the River Tweed.

Herring aid

Herring fishing was once one of Scotland's strongest industries, 2,000,000 barrels of herring having been sold at its peak around 1910–12. Herring also feature prominently in Scottish poems and folk songs and they even inspired the novel *The Silver Darlings* by Neil Gunn.

Old religion

Scotland boasts the oldest ecclesiastical building in Britain, a 6th-century cell on Eilach an Naoimh, one of the Garvellach Islands, off the coast of Argyll.

Cairngorm beauty

Cairngorm quartz is a crystal of smoky-brown or yellow colour, named after the range of Scottish mountains in which it is found.

Cairngorm beast

Ben MacDhui, the highest peak of the Cairngorms, lays claim to its own Yeti known, rather unimaginatively, as the 'Big Grey Man'.

A rough wooing

When the Pictish king Nechtan
admired the beauty of her eyes,
St Triduana plucked them out and
sent them to him, speared on a thorn.
During the Middle Ages people would
visit St Triduana's Well in Restalrig
(now part of Edinburgh) seeking a
cure for their eye complaints.

The Book of Kells

The Book of Kells, one of the
finest illuminated manuscripts to
have survived from the Celtic period,
is thought to have been started and
possibly completed at Iona Abbey,
even though it now rests
in Trinity College, Dublin.

Old school ties

Fettes School in Edinburgh includes British Prime Minister Tony Blair, the author Ian Fleming, and Fleming's most famous creation, 007 James Bond, amongst its illustrious alumni.

Lost clan

The 'Lost Clan' is the name given to the descendants of the elite Scottish guard which once served the French monarchy. In 1525 members of this guard were caught in blizzards while crossing the alps and decided to settle there. It is believed that members of the 'Lost Clan' still inhabit the area.

Should auld acquaintance be forgot

Scotland's most famous song, 'Auld Lang Syne', literally translates as 'Old Long Ago', and is still sung at Hogmanay across the world.